Under Moon and Sun

This is an IndieMosh book

brought to you by MoshPit Publishing
an imprint of Mosher's Business Support Pty Ltd

PO Box 4363
Penrith NSW 2750

indiemosh.com.au

A catalogue record for this work is available from the National Library of Australia

https://www.nla.gov.au/collections

Title:	Under Moon and Sun
Subtitle:	A Collection of Poems
Author:	Harford, Catherine (1976–)
ISBNs:	9781922703088 (paperback) 9781922703095 (hardback)
Subjects:	POETRY/Australian & Oceanian; Love & Erotica; Inspirational & Religious; Nature

Cover concept by Catherine Harford.

Cover layout by Ally Mosher at allymosher.com.

Cover images used under licence from Fiverr.

All other elements under licence from Adobe Stock.

Also by Catherine Harford:

They Gave Me Truth

Under Moon and Sun

A Collection of Poems

By
CATHERINE HARFORD

For Lily and Jack
My little stars that fell down
From the heavens

Contents

Seasons of Love

Seasons of Hurt

Seasons of Armament and Reflection

Seasons of Celebration

Seasons of Love

Elegant Tidings

Elegant tidings
To a moon driven site
Seeding the pretence
That dissolves the defence

It disputes nothing
Till there's something of value
That rivets your sky

Stars
And blasts of singing
Nature ringing
In your ears

And the tears
Which tell you
Are so real
In the scheme of things

So essential
And mind blowing

Pan and Piper

My woodland nymph
Your divine femininity
Echoes rhythms
Of lush spring
Your shadowy paths
Of flowers and grass
That billow softly
In a cool breeze

The boughs of trees
That keep us in shade
And pattern us with
The play of the sun

I follow you silently
Breathe in your essence
And wonder at
Your supernatural presence

And as the god and king
Of all natural things
I stand bewitched
Beholden
Wishing to mould you
To my form

Making the play of lovers
As I whisper all over your body
The truth of magnetic touch
With the heavenly realisation
That I need you oh so much

Capture me
Tell me you believe I'm real
Then I'll show you just how good
Life was meant to feel

Evolution

Whisper me a timeless tune
A devotional cry of worship
Desperate to be touched
In our holy crevice

An unmistakable heartbeat
That shudders just for you

Soft and heavy
Urgent and frightened
Spinning in stellar proportions
Designed in windswept motion

All that you hear
All that is near
Stirs stimulative battlement

Dancing the dance of monkeys
Evolution has taught us well

An instinct cloaked in ritual
Nude beneath this hairy vest
I see it all the time now

Astral travel beckons
Planes of terrestrial energy
Outer universe filament
That's where I want to go

C'mon baby baby
I choose you to be my craft

Ti Amo

Troubador shittim
My testament to thee
Kiss my hand
Kiss my arm
Kiss my lips

Showstopping shilly-shally
Shrouded in pyrexia
The things you do to me

Your pythagoras method pyxis
Your pussy puzzle Qu'ran
The birthplace to our thinking
Kept up the thirst in drinking

Praise be beer
As I nibble your ear
Re-echo ancient rhythms
Past loves are calling

A smaller scent
To where, to what
Cavetto piazza pretence

Sense me now
The lights are fading
Tell me how
Your love is jading

And I want to summon the spell
We make this art so well

Our Chile pine candelabra
Sacred charinga citation

How bless'ed both we are

This Lovers' Potion

Levitate this heart o' mine
Tell me that I'm feeling fine
Flee the focus of the glare
Wanting your soul, not your mind

Crab-dancing and swinging
Your bosoms are jiggling
Feel this sensation wriggling
Towards you on par

Open up your thighs
Emit to me all your sighs
Creep in to the crevice
Lavish deep my pelvis
If your eyes start to lose their focus
I'll know we're somewhere near

The last thing that you'll hear
Is the orgasmic lust
Ejaculating unison
Cataclysmic twosome
Heading straight
For the stratosphere

Awakening brand new souls
Inspiring gods of love
Energy in a frenzy
Neritic moons and potions

Let the magic wash over you
Desperate desire for more
Rainbow python carousal
Lover evermore

And your dancing drives me crazy

World Surveyor Man

The goose that laid
The golden egg
Fell into my arms
And I wept
Into the night time

The Gander Prince
He watched me wince
Over and over
Whilst clinging to
My four-leafed clover

His seven wings
Were beating fast
For the concept that
I never grasped
Whispering from the pages
A myth set down in ages

And so the Prince
He cast his eye
Sending healing
To the sky
Landing on
All those in need
A feeling that
They longed to heed

The Swan Goddess
Honked aloud
A lover that
Was far too proud
To share his hands
To share his feet
His horse's hooves
Pounding on the street

What gold the pirates
Wish to plunder
The desire that brought them
All down under
While mushrooms sprout
And falcon's fly
A look that came
Deep from his eye

The moon she rose
As suns did set
And time was there
To aid and abet
Hoping somewhere
Upon the hours
He'd find the means
To restore their powers

The night time closed
The sun came up
He looked at me
And filled my cup
Ruffled feathers
My ears still ringing
Had the angels been yelling
Or where they really singing?

And so we set
Upon an arc
That led us straight
Into the park
The water gleamed
The forest glistened
Left to ponder
And to listen

About the score
This wavering door
That leads to a world
Offering so much more
Faery queens
Sacred dreams
The purring cat
That got the cream

The mountains echoing
With so much laughter
Of warmth and love
And happily ever after
With the help of Duna
And Lady Maya
We were able to take things
So much higher

Flowers scattered
On the rock
We heard the crow
From the golden cock
Nature's beauty
Rainbow showers
A place to bask
In peace for hours

And each time that
He held my hand
My heart did jump
And I thought of Pan
My lover doing all he can
My beautiful World Surveyor Man

The Jagged Bone

Graciously we extend ours
To each other
To receive the bliss
That comes amidst
A wealth to share
In dreams and love
And a rhythm repair

Questing the notion
Sweet, sensory potion
Tides running in and out
We're dazzled by the ocean

Sparkles and opaque vision
A world of indecision
Believe iconoclasm
We're human after all

And with our daily bread
Love gathers in our stead
With luck to one
And hope to some
A travelling deep neurectomy

Frogmarch lissajous devotion
Cursed by all-believing
Culture deft deceiving
While those around us pray

Whittle Mercury malignance
Dreaming dreams of desistance
Dragon's fire liquified
The longest time of day

Potential cold resistance
Dance your method madly
Determinative path persistence
Basket wicker weaving
Trying to get home

Eventually we all call in
And touch the jagged bone

The Temple on the Hill

Is it the way that I walk?
The way that I talk?
The way that I worship
And the way that I baulk?

Neveah arrested
The balance tested
Was there ever meant
Such a divide
Tween the right and wrong
Night time and song

Captive in conscience
To free and belong
Heaven in parchment
Sent into bliss
Awaiting angel's kiss

Caressing and caressed
The breeze blows up my dress
As I seek out yonder castle
Awaiting this cosmic parcel

Grant me this wish
Patience, gratitude, dismiss
Yearning and discerning
Left cold and baptised
After summer swings
In the desire for all things

No rock unturned
No faery faint fortune
Accepting the hand of god and goddess

I used to live in that sacred temple
Out there upon the hill

Now I wait, longing to serve
Your every command and will

Night Prayers

I crept along the outskirts of town
Up this street, down that
Pitter-pattering under well-lit streetlights
That glowed golden in the night

I wandered, who knows where
Glimpsing into bright windows
Sensing a taste of someone else's home
Empty canvases of perfectly strange
arrangement

I climbed higher, further
Stretching legs, heartbeats and thoughts
Expanding on breath and wellness
As the night breeze tousled my hair

Soaking up the starlight
The palm tree silhouette
Dancing on the winds of future dreams
sewn
All we forget and choose to forget

I walked until I saw you
The outline of your face
And though I couldn't see it exact
The sense I could not erase

I ran straight down the hill
And begged the gods until
They promised, soon, I'd hold you close
If that would be my will

I screamed it to the sky
My longing by the by
My soul on fire, my heart alight
My lover till I die

Settling into soon
One night, beneath the moon
You'll appear in my life, against all odds
And I'll recall the tune

One perfect day, they cried
The day that you decide
You'll be out walking, something's calling
you
My early dying bride

The Liaison

I'll meet you in
These sacred planes
Where you cleanse
My dirty face
Esoteric taste
Of fraudulent spiritual liaison

Must be imagination
This subtle energy persuasion
Healing me in transoms
Earthly meditative positions
Oscillating emissions
From a space of progressive thought

This positivity you've taught
Holds boundless possibility
Within me and here with me
Your electric blue radiation
Hovers where I learn to see

Clasping potential unisons
And letting go of notions
Closing in on oceans
That held us in abyss
Awaiting lovers' bliss
And pending explosive sensations

The time when we find our kiss

The Harvest

Caught between sunlight and moonlight
But there's a time when sun and moon
Build space long enough
For us to face the love
That runs between us

For friends, and friendship
Are the pastoral key

Till this energy
Wait until it's ripe
Then pluck it
Pull it up

Nature's love and resource
Harvested in its due course

Found for the tenderness
Of the peaceful, nurtured elements
Of coexistence and patience

Merrymaking

Merry are the folk
Who join with love
The trickling of laughter
Serendipity
Smacks of sensuality
As your fingers trace over places
Too rich to erase
With pandemonium

The dandelion effect
And the deepest respect
Of tribalism

Hunting me down
In this holy prism
Devouring my tears
And making it clear
That you wish to go deep
Sweep me off my feet

Baiting me as you're waiting
To snare me in your web
With devastating precision

My heart skips
As I feel your lips
Sucking up the flavour
The essence of the energy
Of all the love
You give to me

The taste of romance
Alive and tantalising
All the fantasising I need
Right here

As I stare into your eyes
We bid this new surprise
Of all that our lives
Have come to realise

In the magic
That we make
Together

The Thief

Like a beggar in the night
I broke in
And stole her heart

She rewarded me solace

We crafted an energy
That mystified the night
The stars shuddered
She sang my delight

Wandering through my motion
The destiny of my home
Belief that she knows everything
Muffled in a sigh

She whispers me such poetry
Frightening the senses
The urgency of responsibility
What is it I'm meant to do?

She accuses me
And she woos me
I'm left naked and raw

She feeds so many others
And I wonder what I'm for

Loaded to the hilt
The devilish flavour of ecstasy
She radiates right next to me
And now she's got the best of me

Golden Locks and Keys

The inward pressure of performance
Impressive rites
To the passage of your time

Politic refined
Minimal damage
From the crashest course
In time, space, blind refined
Do it double time
Not knowing naught
But the feeling sublime
Welfare of a duet
Fraught with love and crime

Mine to be away with
To say with
To give forth
And sway with
An angel so mighty
Of love and kindness
And heartiness

The Australian method
Of being humoured into
Dust bowls of devotion

Oceans, craters, edges and shelves
Of earthly crustaceans and plates
A few minor quakes
And species in between

To make it seem so real baby
So real to feel and hold you
And not hold out on you

You have me all the same
Like a toy of human proportions
To meet your golden hues
What I do and chase
To make breeze face you
Soft, cool breeze
Ease, you make and free

Key in, delivering a signal
Of advent fantastic making
Shaking the debris
Obliterating the burnt hollowness
With your friendliness
You key in the restitution
Of forgiveness
Blessings amounted
Accounted for

Tear it down
Not to know that and score
Wrecked in momentous gesture
Of illegitimate unknowing

But where else to free
To be the free me
And giving jealousy, is that bad?

You just drive me there
Unawares and good times
Bless unto you
Clean the refrigerator
In this hot country

Try to take else
For the ritual of togetherness

Tenderness
Your wont of being
Bless'ed child

Your Christ-pose bequeathed
With golden locks and keys

Celestial Love

The moon turns tonight
Sheds new light
On the womb
That gave new life

As you roll over
She caresses your thigh
Lifts you high
Into the warmth of the night
Lovers' flight
Soaring everywhere

She touches you there

Surrendering your shadowed thoughts
The stars a blurry hail of diamonds
Showering the senses
Blending into the universe

You are one
With all or none
Careful to breathe the love
That lives for you

Your circle unites it
And she delights in it
When you turn tonight
And the world turns just right
All in space, tonight

The Hues of You

Steep yourself
Too deep in femininity

You may lose yourself
To the tightened scope
The blend and love that exist
The tables turned

What do I have to offer
When the blue light shines
On me?

Enough passion
Or shades of anger
Maybe earth to draw me back
Draw me in

Solidify the tones
Of a grander heartbeat
Right into the soul

Can I offer love and sunshine
To appease you?

To warm the ripening harvest
And a pearly moonlight
Soft and tender
Remind you of heaven
The violet, the blue
The hues of you

Where do I lend
My humanity?

Their pink light reminds me
Not sure if it blinds me
But it's true, they do want me here

For Dallas

As we build up and break away
The fragile shards of our existence
We throw caution to the wind
And jump into the circle
For the crazy chance
We might dance
Till daylight

Nightlights spotting our souls
From out of the darkness
That beyond our confusion
We might find each other
If only for a short while

To revive ourselves
In the shelter
Of a grand existence
That belongs to us
On this night

Stories Old and New

Dream and stay
Love to play
As paint dries and cloudy skies
Keep storms at bay

Lightening ripples
Maybe water
Will whisk us away
With the flow

I'll flood your caverns
With the endless source
The driest year
Is really only fuel

Foraging fire
Sister o'mine
Wait and see
If we can't finally be

Higher than the rain
Than the trees
Than dreams
That tickle our feet
Just like stories of old and new

Summer Love

Silence is a crest
And I behest the time
You choose to dance across
My dirt-field

Sealed in time
Rock and rhyme
Blessed in fire
Beer and dowry

Smell me into the season

Giving me reason
To feel the heat
Violence retreat
Betwizzled by the ash and smoke

I love the way
And I'll definitely stay
All summer long

Measure for Measure

Measure for measure
The by-line for pleasure
Is a world-weary heart
And a well-hidden treasure

Don you your scuba gear
Honesty abounds so sincere
Till you sink deep into her waves
And gasp the unholy sight of fear

Waiting be a system of mine
And luck will come with time
But when you land on foreign ground
Show to me a glorious sign

For laughter's what I know best
And the sun truly ever sets in the west
And till we have no more excuses
We will always be put to the test

So lover of mine, be friendly
And guide me ever so gently
Come time for the glorious rainbow
showers
You'll know just how to send me

The Daily News

Lessons are a taste
And the taste of being
Is a blessing of seeing
Kneading the existence
Of a palatable life

Paint more
And steal some glances
Frank transparence
Of another's soul

Hold your world
Into a great screen
See what it is seen
When the great beauty takes hold

Fold me here
And I'll place the daily news
Into your time

Eyes On

The lightest trail
I'm feeling my way
Your touch
Tracing its way
Across my face
To a place
All of your own
That you designed
And I contributed to
Making this zone
Tingle and live

Eyes on, baby
Eyes on

Eyes on my prize

I terrorise to feel your . . . mmm

I believe, kind sir
That t'were it not an act of fate
Hath done in bringing us thus far
To this place
Where I find you hovering
Shivering
Shovelling boredom in droves, baby
All day

Criminal Fantasy

Exponential
The ongoing of one
From the other

Lover to lover
Friend to brother
Sealed with a rhyme
That's systematically fading
Beliefs that are essential
And a zest that is waning

Come at it more
Again from your centre
And if you're a real whore
Best it from agenda

For yours is the real deal
If you believe what I say
Cause when you deliver
The mind is a dull sway

But if you know better
Show me a kink
Think me out
Blink it in
And pray like hell
That the felling is twinkling

Within you I'm sinking
Your soul I am drinking

And through it all is a waxed place
A pungent trace
Of criminal fantasy

The lover in you
Is the land I have to see

Hey Baby

A lovely expectation
Not quipped
With jealousy or mirth

Just the birth
Of a new, unconventional way
To be at bay
And shine
Into another day

When I say, hey baby
I mean *hey*

Roots

Fell into a deep sleep
And when I woke
You spoke in greensleeves

Golden harness
Saddle me now

Hold that moment
The cow only appeared
And the moon jumped too soon

Rattle the soil
For your roots grow here now

For Eros

My dear Seraph
Acutely aware
Of burgeoning back flips

Sedentary freeze frames
Are falling out of the sky

Dense matter to abscond
Is the heartfelt reckoning
Believing this to be heavenly

The place I find
The leaves of the poverty tree
Attempting regrowth

I try not to leave
To feel the upward rush
Of your wing'ed thrust

Sensoralites awaiting

Heavenly Love

Even more than ever
I begin to unfold

Unravel the mysteries that lie within
Longing to be spoken
With an ancient, unused tongue

Come to me, come through me
Ensue me till I can take no more

Then take me to your sacred planes
And feed me on the nourishing riches
That abound there

Lend me your prayer
That I may rise again
And sing untainted
Dance unabated
In the liveliest of ways

I'll give my all
Till I fall to the floor
Kiss your aerial feet
And plead with you for more

To follow through my servitude
While you guide me home

The Ticket

Give me a ticket, baby
Fear is flagging my flight
Tell me, cause I'll help you
Any way I can

The tuition of my life circle
Swinging to the left
Are you standing ajar
On the right?

I thought and I read some
Maybe a little too deeply
But I thought to bury you sweetly
In the gorges of my body

Heaving, hovering
Into the recesses
Of soul space
Closely tagging
The trips of desire
That lead you with me

As your voice goes deeper
And sinking
Oh, oh, falling
So quickly
And landing
Inside the pink cushion
Of my own flesh

The senses of sensation
As your being swells to meet me
To greet me
To heat me, baby
Up and over
Into a dimensional drive
Of the newest flight

A space light
Reflecting through
The seas tonight

Green and Blue

Leave it for me
Take it easy some today
And wait

I'm contemplating my way
Into a foraging plain

Taking the grains
That fruitful scent beckons

Tasting more
Wanting more
Feeling your presents
Inject me with life
Twofold and a hundred score

Needing the shore
To wave me in

The essence of sin forgiven
In a natural spring

As green and blue
Transport you
To a new form

The Sage

Letting up on the emptiness

Followed you here
Cleft of all that self-hatred ruins

I long to stand tall in your presence

When I feel that magic
Adrift in my soul
The energy of the world
Is brilliantly told

And strangely, just as each has life-love to
bring
Somehow you're the only one hearing it

Seasons of Hurt

Heaven Bound

Serendipity
A fractural key
When the lapwings are squawking
Get away, get away

Let her be
Afraid
Her holy day

A quarter moon waning
A fresh bleed
A treble tremolo
Of soft vibration

Emanating
From deep within

Caught over frying pans
Humbling servility
The queen at her best
Sequester put to test

Plateau of throes
To be heaven bound

Sanctions

The days bleed into one another now
The sanction of my senses
Has left me idle
Not so much moving backward
But with no will
To go forward

Numbness is welcomed
Purely as a change
From the self-imposed hurt
That runs rampant in my soul

Here, I don't cry
I do not pine
Nor wallow
Nor scorn or abate

In its collective stead
Acceptance resounds
And somewhere I opt
Not to fight that

Too long now have I wept inside
Though I wish the truth lay
In stronger favour
Of the courage to let go

Lo, no weaker faculty
Currently plays a part in me

Is forgetting the same
As letting go?

So much easier
To simply forget
Pass over and realize the end
But it comes back for you
It always comes back

You never really forget
Only the liar forgets
The fool chooses not to

Tea and Solace

Are you offering me
Tea and solace?
Do you break bread with me?
Or wish me as your stead?

I coil up to dream
In such golden hues
Of forest in sunshine
And wonder again
If it's my time
Or a puppet show of feeling

Where I host the strings
But know nothing
Of the content

Do I bare such little resemblance
To the contact?

When you react
I can't re-act

The devilish slew performance
Trapped here in my innocence
No escape in sight

The sun comes forth
Again and again
Longing to stay and play
Brighten up our rainy day

As she haughtens true love
I exalt like a dove
Yet I can't see the horizon for the trees

And the bliss that's amiss
All evident in Pan's kiss
Has brought me down to my knees

As I long for a time
Far before our current crime
Where I was free to wish upon
Such faery dreaming

The Young Hag

Playing on doll scenes
And mandatory growth
Caught between a ken oath
And a burning need
To be the one

Come about in night times
The moon does not approve

Why stuff the light of balance
Into my notebook?

Re-reading canters and gestures
Semi-profane dialogue
Groggy from the headspace
Laced with jealousy

And seeing is believing
But knowing
Is a time-honoured performance
Settled in soulful truth

Wench seizes
And youth wrenched

You young hag

What giddiness and delight
Beneath a tarnished mainstay?

Hearts away from the settlement
Of negatory affusion
Sifting through the petals
That may one day bring my peace

The War

I could feel blood
Could taste it
Death coursing
Under my skin
Shredding my nerves
To pieces

Icing the burns
Until the only sensation
Is that of defeat
To one who
Has greater control
Of your tenements
Than any lord of the land
You thought you might be

And a genteel sing-song voice comes
And whispers, "Leave, just leave"

But the wind that delivers it
Carries it away
The force of hatred and fear
So strong
That it shall not be heard
Not here
Not today

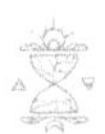

Evening swells
The full moon
Binds the seal

Sickly sweet
Will time be now
Oh
No open door
No exodus of war

Not now
Not for tonight

The Incarnate

Look at my ring of rosies
Look at my artful posies
Telling me not to weep
Into this tit

Floral passings
The blue fairy wren skips
She is all of brown
A royal carpet
Of ashen green

Could it be the Eden socage?
A blueprint of evaporative history
A fairytale birthright
The poorest of porn stars

Egyptian incarnate
Power rotating
The moon on tilt
Energy spilling, baby

Is it real
Or is it bullshit?

The Water Dragon

The Water Dragon spilling his tears
Fulfilling the gifts that were owing for
years
In a time and a place
That chartered pure space
Lest condemnation stain
Such a fair face

No pause for regret
With destiny set
The misshapen cruise
That left everyone wet

The dams overflowed
The waterways blowed
The parched and dry earth
Half-drenched and aglow

Why, why?! Cried all men
Why why come again?
Foolish and curt
Cooped up in their pen

They'd lost all meaning
As the tears came a'streaming
Their ignorance the menace
Spilled from strict ego preening

It's us, it's us
The narcissist lust
That kept man bound
To much lower ground

The squirming
The writhing
Endeared by their striving
As each footstep came apart
And led them straight into the dark

"Who'll free us?" they cried
So empty inside
Their fear the flavour
Of what form their saviour?

The Dragon comes, weeping
Tears mounting and seeping
Refreshing waterholes
Cleansing all the lost souls

The Earth's spirits he did muster
With divine, wondrous lustre
The mystical love for all
With each tear that falls

Healing the ways
Bidding us come
Having us dream up
The bright, blazing sun
But until men
Finally see
That they are not all
His tears will fall

The Dragon's tears, they will fall

For Loved Ones Lost

Bless your heart
Here we start
You're over there
I fall apart

Laying my claim
Pastoral blame
You are my home
If it's all the same

Try not to trip
With such feeble grip
From all that was borne
Of body and lip

Smell me, I muster
For all that may bluster
Is frugal and past
Still doused in this lustre

It radiates for me
Though you'll never see
The love that we shared
Will always fly free

So cry me a river
As faeries deliver
The faint hope of all
That comes again never

And when I stumble blindly
Please, treat me kindly
Perhaps, when all is done
You'll come back to find me

The Darkest Night of the Soul

As she sits and sways
Gently rocking, crying
And wondering for the 'enth time
That she was chosen to endure
This endless battle of terror
Besieged within her soul

The nightmare of existence
With every waking breath
No place for cover
No one to help her
And no end in sight

None but her to deliver thoughts
On this forsaken, endless night

Attributing a reason
To every chemical plume
So much that every season
Fills a moment in this room

She sits and stares at nothing
And everything to bear
Wishing death for the millionth time
She knows she'll never dare

A criminal state of being
Prison-bound for years
No rest in one's own solitude
A daily shed of tears

And as the walls start tumbling
She's looking for a sign
For the only relief, her god's own touch
Can fill her in this time

Suddenly her conscious opens
She's thrilled to be alive
As an energy gently strokes her face
And tells her not to cry

"This path that you are taking
Is ancient in its score
Only the bravest, heartiest warriors
Have travelled here before

Close your weary eyes now
Try to get some sleep
When you reach the sun again
Wisdom's company you'll keep

Fool you not the length of time
That passes by you now
But count your blessings, heed your
thoughts
Be grateful this is how

Those who survive the underworld
Are only but a few
You will survive, you'll be alive
Imagine all that you can do?

A force of cosmic energy
Will see you to this end
And with the lasting memory
Fate will be your friend

Pity not the journey
The archetype is yours
A power held by very few
Will open you your doors

Believe that you were chosen
This is how it will be
Angels driving notions
Especially for thee

Be grateful here and ever
Fill your heart with joy
What every human longs for
Will be your living toy

Dragon scent of sweetness
A mystery divine
Never lose sight of the end, child
All it takes is time"

Keep Climbing

The things I know
That which I love
Will keep making me sad
Depressed or angry
In cycles

In circles

I must keep dancing through
The mists
Till I reach
The promised land

Rising up
To the heavens
And stars
Once more

The Cult

That's right
We worked out a way
To embed ourselves
In the deepest recesses
Of your mind

In the very essence
Of your soul

So what?

So we worked it out
It worked
You're still fooled
By the meaninglessness of it
And downtrodden
By the emptiness

Your spark is measured
Your bliss is fractured
True to the word
In case you hadn't heard
We found a way
To covet your life

You found god
And asked for little more
All the more fool you
Not to read
Between the lines

The answers were there
All along

Don't you care?
We fooled you with the completeness
Of reckless, stereotypical behaviour
And still you look to the saviour
For all of your answers

As vampires dance
And feast on the pain
Of all you offer
On your knees
Begging for relief
We'll take it

But in the wake of this transaction
Be sure to attribute devotion
For the bond is now eternal
And there's no going back
Without waking up
To the retribution

A damned solution

Strange Delights

What strange delight
Finds me burning
In my chamber?

A yearning so strong
Willing her man
To come and claim her

She frets the time
When suitors seek out
His affection

Her jealousy
So easily
Marks detection

Toiling with
The belief inside
That he'll even stay

For all the pain
Far too many games
Stain from day to day

War No More

I don't want to sit and not write
About sisters and soldiers
Brothers and lovers
Who once were and still are
And separate me
A hundred million lifetimes

Me and my true self
When this is my time
My chosen time

As I sit idle
And let it all flow through me
Not to see the story breathe
The way we chose it to be

This magic inspires
And frightens me
Into a place I'd once believed
I wouldn't ascend from

Watch me, I cower
I hide from your love
And time slips on
I watch it, you, fly from me

Poison Arrows

You disarm me so well
For that, I celebrate
Laying down my weapons
When weapons cause destruction
But devastation abounds
At my feet

Pick up the pieces
How to do what he says
When your life is broken in two

Still, there is you
Reminding me
Blinding me with truth
From deep in my soul
Reflecting the nature of yours

Our blood
Our ties
Eyes locked on the same prize

Show me some reprieve
From this desolation
We both cry
We scream
And yell sounds
Into another time frame

But our barriers
They're strong
Our pleas don't escape
Our echoes pierce us
Like poisoned arrows

The flight of sparrows
Flutters our final hope
And will surely take us home

The Funeral Rite

For all of life's tragedies
Oh, how wondrous it can be!
Tied up in strife
A heartfelt filagree

The lilies, the ferns
That dip and sway
Recalling daydreams
Of a better day

Wrapped up in grief
Bleakness dissipates
With the settling
Of cosmic dust

Starshine transformed
Fire and energy
Radiating
Recreating colour anew

Brighter than
You've ever seen

Come, visit me in dreams
I'll welcome you home
Comfort your fears
And take the pain away

I won't turn you away
Not today

Not on this sad, sad day

A Bridge Too Far

Oh my god
You've done it now

You've opened the floodgates
Of retribution
Your stupid solutions
Are flagrant restitutions
Emblazoned with resonance
Of a sewer-strung fear

Wasting space
And a lack of grace
To the word you speak
The control you seek

Lest some evil trick
Fell the forest of redemption
You've sown in your mind

But you hold the axe, dear

Keep swinging
The shadow's retreating
And nature's calling your bluff

If you won't believe in anything else
Look over your shoulder
The desert is tough

Restrict your soul's flight
As you pluck your rectrix
But recumbent days are over
This recusant is out

The sequestrate bleeding
Let someone else mop it up
Your wish to dishonour
Will someday backfire

Pity you
And the day

Tempting Fate

Turn and face the hand of time
Unravelling truth with every rhyme
As something sticks from olden tricks
And feelings buffer the state of crime

Agony is your bread and butter
Twisting good health with all you utter
The speed of sound accrues every pound
Of flesh that you hope will gutter

Bleeding hearts lie far ashore
Skeletons peek through every door
And sticks and stones come with
megaphones
In the hope all else will be just as sore

Do you like to see us on our knees?
Squirming discomfit, ill at ease?
For you may jest, but this ghastly test
Means such little forest for the trees

Try as I might to out-wait it
I'm bogged down and filled with the hate
of it
With tears in your eyes and little disguise
You mock your own fate with the weight
of it

So burdensome and desperately sad
Deriding those who're not bad
But the fact is you waste with imperious
haste
All that which could make you feel glad

I love you but I do have to wonder
At your measure when you bring all
asunder
The storm in your cup fills you right up
As you choose to rage on and to thunder

My hope for you is all but gone
With your refusal to ever move on
No time for life's sweetness, opting only
for bleakness
If your choices in the end were all wrong

Good luck with your disharmony
So blind you will just never see
And maybe death's kiss is all that's amiss
In your pale bid to finally fly free

Devil in Disguise

He bid me come
Into the night
He waited in
The soft moonlight
With quivering hands
He held me tight
My devil in disguise

His touch rang out
With promises strong
A passion bound
In everlong
But I knew that
I could be wrong
My devil in disguise

Mist descended
Through the trees
A rhythmic dance
That came with ease
Either he, or I
Or both to please
My devil in disguise

His sturdy form
Was like a tower
As he took me deep
In the witching hour

And I surrendered
All my power
To my devil in disguise

To feel his hands
Upon my face
To lose myself
In his embrace
To smell his smell
And taste his taste
My devil in disguise

And though this might
Be over soon
I take him once more
By the moon
And savour the way
He makes me swoon
My devil in disguise

For now you are
My only dream
My mighty thrust
My fervent cream
You'll never hear
My nightmare scream
My devil in disguise

I know that I've
Been here before
So many times
Left cold and raw
I've learned this dance
I know the score
My devil in disguise

I know you'll leave
Before it's light
I know that I'll
Be not quite right
But right now I need you
In the night
My devil in disguise

The owl's soft hoot
Is all I'll hear
As you promise to
Be always near
But you'll not come again
My dear
My devil in disguise

I'll howl down every
Darkened door
Until I feel
Your touch no more
But use me now
That's what I'm for
My devil in disguise

Twelve Dimensions

Dying to get home
Trying to get home
In any way, shape or form
Twelve dimensions picked out
But I'm stuck here in third
Listening to the frequencies
Of what has and hasn't been heard

Tell me lover
What will it be?
Last time I checked
Nothing is free

The price
Is sky high
We're failing
To see

That nothing in this life
Anymore
Is free

Instant Karma

Inspiring the pity of the gods
Unable to intervene
Watching helplessly
As you burn up
Burning alive
In hellish fire

And in your reflection
You see the empty shell
Feed the remnants
The pile of ash
Reduced to nothing

Dorian Gray
Couldn't hold a candle
To the evidence
Of your handiwork

Etching itself
Across your face
Like a blade of the heavens
Had wounded you

As you search through the dust
The sooty remnants
Of your soul
And find not one spark

No happy ember
From which a phoenix
Could even rise
And deliver you

Just the cold realisation
That this complete damnation
Was of your own making
According to the laws of karma
As all you put out there
Comes back for you

The King, The View of Things

The king persists in his view of things
This all-encompassing canvas
With careful consideration for
Each colourful strand
Each skilfully devised stitch

The picture, he knows
Is as seemingly perfect
But he sees it in his own way
And in this he knows
That maybe all
Will not do as much

For this measure
He must tax the poor
For what giveth a divine christening
Other than the divine eyes of God?

Each man passing over
A levee of testament and truth
The willing soul
As the aura of God himself
Might descend upon them
Emissivity for a precious few

What price the punishment
For one's own design of sight?

The forbearing is such
Living in an existence
Which gradually fades away
And is masked by a gravitational pull

It wills earthbound momentum
For enrapture of such superlative gifts
Passed into each human's possession
With the accordance of a celestial
handiwork

And the product?

The divergence into
A demanding regime
Impressed upon
By an ungracious tenement
Of social servants
Tempered only by that
Which they expect is true

The right thing to do

Too fractious for a weaker man
Such waste for any mind
That wells a despairing
Tressure about himself
As the world looks on
With a burgeoning anarthria
The individual choice
To do or not to do

Afraid of that which may come
And a desperate sense of inadequacy

As some may delve
To penetrate one's overwrought shield
There spells a gluttonous message
Of deliverance about one's own self-
structure
Clubbed from the inside to the out

Such heady work

Frightening arraignment of
Forespent neuro-invasion
A battle of minds
Never to be won

Maybe for some
When the work is done

For the greater balance
Requires a shock of diaspora
A destiny of emollient self-imposed exile
A chance to live and breathe the word
Outside of the dogma

Personal release
Social retreat
Universal harmony
As a stake in tomorrow's world

Frowning, he can see the truth
He knows there is little to be done

The free world will see
To its own divination

Hart's Nightstand

As the gods took up my hands
And the forest bustle bore Hart's
nightstand
Were we free to love as genesis in the
making

Now with such ancient ribbons
I come to bind your rhythms
But the present is far stickier than
expected

And the hex on my love
Has me trite sunken glove
As I fight to be free
You collar superficies

Still the radiance you ask of her
Keeps you bound as her master
And I wonder what good
My heart's sappan wood
Will do once it flows free

Only timing will tell
Should I happen under spell
And find a new space
For it all to take place
The lotus and the maiden
Assure nothing is forsaken
And the story will breathe as it needs

Where the forest floor
Will reveal so much more
And blanket my dreams in its leaves

Until Then

When shalt thou dream of better days?
When wilt thou love turn hate rephrase?
Bomblasted by thine heart a'fixed
Lost hopes cried less of sunsets be'twixt

Thou shalt not burn mine heart aflame
If all days ne'er do much the same
Crystalise in thine bed
And clever undone of all thou hast said

T'is nary dusk that falls on this
Yet declarations remain amiss
Till the next life

Winter Lament

A soft and summary
Woodland breeze
Used to put
My mind at ease

Now the swell
Of winter chill
Grips me out
Upon this hill

As I extrude
Every drop
Of love spelled out
Upon this crop

Damn this harvest
To its end
Should I never feel
The sun again

The Corner of the World

Sitting at the edges
Of the corner
Of the world
Trusting soon
It will all unfurl
And I'll finally know
The taste of freedom
Once more

What's it all been for?
The feeling, the thrill
Of life, of love
Brief glimpses in time
Memories carried on a breeze
Of the moments I felt at ease
The dance steps I followed
The sun, the stars and the moon
The drumbeats and rhythms
The colours that lifted me up
So high

I just want that
I need that
To feel that
To remember what it's like
To be that high

Circling above the earth
Sweeping up and over
Clouds soft and billowing
The heavens my pillow
A divine place
To rest and recover

To recall the truth
Of what and who I am

As real as the earth
As cosmic as the universe
As bright as the face of the gods
Shining, oscillating
Pulsating, reverberating
Drifting through dreams
And realms that seem
To be full of love and laughter
And the something that I'm after

Once upon a time
You bade me follow
Now will you always evade me?
When I gave everything I had
To feel a part of you
To believe in my worth
To feel out your girth
Of monumental figurement

Yet here I sit
In my corner of the earth
Waiting
Waiting
Still anticipating
Your return

I thought I was your water nymph
Your rushing river
Swollen and ripe
Forcing and cutting my way
Through the territory
That emanates
Your significance

I thought you'd be there
After the fall
After cascades and tirades
Where pools trickle over mountains
Where fountains of spring
Dazzle with regeneration
And the metaphoric sensation
Of your holiness
Could crumble me
To dust
And our union
Of fire and lust
Would shake the world
To its core

Yet here I sit
With wit and woe
Wondering if
I'll ever know
The relief
As giant eagle wings
Swoop down and enfold
Hold me and carry me
Through energy bands
Through rainbow sands
Into the wonderment of your love

Sitting, waiting
At the edges
Of the corner
Of your world
Eyes scanning the skies above
Wrapped up in dreams and hope
Believing
One day you'll come

Whose Country?

Dusty reminders
Of trees and leaves
Our wide brown land
Is a chaotic notion of motion

From the ocean
Down the East coast
To a patchwork country
War-torn by
Commercial energy
And the desire
To perpetuate money

To think that when they got here
It wasn't green enough

Does it seem enough
To run another man's land?
And if you claim you own it
Will the earth's powers
Awake you rudely?

Is it possible
You are a quake
In the making?

Whisper me
Are you shaking
In your foundations?

How many nations
Devise planetary rotations?

Gradations of human philosophy
The right to your country
Whole and just

Cover it all with crust
Because bread
Makes the world go round
But it doesn't touch my heart

Doesn't make me feel unlucky
When I'm the one
Who holds a rainbow
In my palm

Delivering
A steadiness
Of flow

Oh, Serpent of the land
Abounding in colour bands
Where everyone understands

We are each a man

Winter's Kiss

Awakening to
Darkening skies
Ruined castles
In jungle disguise
Emerald green
As bright as your eyes
As I seek out winter's kiss

Encloaked in air
Warm to the touch
As heavy as breath
That seems too much
Recalling the heat
Of my lover's touch
As I seek out winter's kiss

Crystal blue
Of threatening seas
Tender softness
Of tropical breeze
An ancient calling
Whispering through trees
As I seek out winter's kiss

Tell me we've
Been here before
Show me through
Your open door

And I will plead
And beg for more
As I seek out winter's kiss

For I long to heal
In your embrace
To travel deep
In darkened space
And cover this moistness
Face to face
As I seek out winter's kiss

No more cold
And lonely nights
Only dizzying
Heavenly delights
A momentum
That was always right
As I seek out winter's kiss

Instead I fumble
Old and lonely
Dreaming dreams
Of if only
Not sure if you
Could ever know me
As I seek out winter's kiss

And so I'll wander
Across the moor
Star-crossed lovers
Who can't be sure
Condemned to accept
That forever more
Shall I seek out winter's kiss

Wednesday's Child

Feeling earth tremors
As time draws on the moisture
Of raindrops fallen
Storm clouds hovering
From so long ago

Wednesday's child
Battling her woe

With winter painting
A snow scene in her heart
Icicles melting slowly
Individual droplets
Patterning a subcontinent

A place to mull over dreams
And hide from the rest of the world
A chance for bad feelings
To unfurl

She cakes it and tries hard
Not hard enough
But to call her bluff
Leaves out by the wayside
Dancing wildly by the bayside

You'll not find her there
She left
She was always gone

She was with him all along

The Witch's Tower

She crept up into her tower
Seeking the eye
That willed her there
Longing to see
The true she
The wild worldly woman
She hungered to free

As dominion cowered
And caved her in
Her presence
Her resonance
Seemed unholy sin

Prodded and pushed
By unfair appraisal
She stumbled, suspended
In her natural ways

For who could forgive
The gifts of a witch?
Unwanted and frightening
So out of place
In a gridlocked world

And so I become
A shadow girl

Cold and suspended
In uncertainty
As the years forged new growth
On the family tree

I am now tolerated
By the skin of my teeth
But there'll come a day

When these ill-fitting shoes
Squeezing at my neck
Shaking my pride

Will be the catalyst
For artistic overdrive

The Neophite

The neophyte hampered her own dealings
Aware of bodies strung with a magic
passion
The gift of majesty encompassed
Took its toll
Driving her to the edges
And ravines of her mind

Whittled down to social performance
Urged to institutionalise
What would they do with her?

What could they do?
Cap in hand, daily, nightly
Riding off into the sunset

Gentlemen speak, Kierkegaard spoke
And that bizarre, random clock chimed

Off she would go
Who would ever know where?
Or if she'd live to see daylight

Skirting the mountains
Streaming the stars
Heavy breath persuasion
She was dreaming it up
Drowning it down

Frowning so deeply
Before rigor mortis set in

A glorious battle
To remain fair

Encumbered by the heat swell
Frozen by minds
And long-gone times
A half-hearted resolution to endure
Making these madness moments
All the more worthwhile

Capturing the sense of freedom
Bottling it up
Savouring it for later
These youthful elixirs
Needed for a time much later
When peace still seems lightyears away

Pieces of Eight

Basking in the warm glow
Of your self-inflated ego
Dazzled and blinded
And constantly reminded
That I am not worthy
To spend time in your proximity

As truth will never bend to be
This shadow that you lend to me
For my heart craves a position
A fair dinkum notion
Of how things really are
You've pushed me oh so far

I waver on the brink
You wish me to walk your plank
And I sink, for sure, beneath the waves
As I hover here in fear

I try to be brave
But just to save myself
I dive in, again and again
Freer as I drown
Or swim without my crown
It's better than dealing with you

This kingdom is rife with theft
Plundering the soul's gold and what's left

An empty shell of virtue
While I never looked to hurt you
Still your stinging state of self
Has you kept up on your shelf

And to do all that you please
Only brings me to my knees
So happily I set out to roam
Fleeing all that you would call home

Your pirate heart lies afeared
And your failure to endear
Forces me out of your zone

Oh Dear (The Pecking Order)

Go ahead and cry into the moonlight
Your insolence keeps you warm
So you can't feel forlorn
Whilst metered chaste living
Rescinds oncoming storms

A perpetuation of half-truths
And all you like is good news
Stand aground your law suit
To snob, condone or refute
At your sniper scope will

Being the grand judge of all and all

To sneer or snicker
And pull the trigger
Of your extractive armament
As the primary cells of all we tell
Must pass your sensitometry
Or flounder in incendiary

For booby traps abound
In far less common ground
The boon of your bonfire boogie
Burning away all of distaste
To coalesce
The finest of grace
And levitate
Only the best we face

For fear of metropolis?
Tackiness?
Salaciousness?
The tardiness
Leading to troublousness?

So vulnerable to snake bite
For the style of sin must be just right
And the skulduggery of your skip zone
Keeps it skin deep

Still the henpecking in your hen run
Makes me want to weep

It's Your Move

The King and Queen
Of the chessboard
Collecting all their pieces

The Queen moves
The Queen moves
Check out their groove

They jig and jive
Oh, so alive
Come aboard, our little pawn

Rattle and roll on
So much more to get done
Preening you for Queendom
If you follow orders well

Come of age
Don't misbehave
Don't stray, little lamb
You're only a pawn, after all

Dispensable
Reprehensible
Oops, how far you thought
You had come

You were just a pawn all along

Kings and Queens shuffle
Make kingdom kerfuffle
You shouldn't be here
It's our game
After all

Checkers and minds
All black and white
Ready to take the fall

The Cold Heart

Clandestine worship
Ah, you're clever
How do you do it?
Leaving me gobsmacked
And bushwhacked

Full of dimension
Too cool for school
Your transition reverie
Has them all in your palm
And they love every second

Bewitching devotion
Love set in motion
The will of one's sex

Fire the cauldron
Boil the brew
All eyes on you

Feed it
Taste it
No one to waste it

Bosom arrested
Monogamy tested
Slutting imagination
Nymphette extraordinaire

Worship me
Down on your knees
I am the goddess
Embodiment of lust
You can't compare

They're dazzled
Under my spell
Utterly irresistible
Because I will it so

The Calamitous Mess

It appears the replication
Is of my own complication
When I know what's to come
Is akin to what's glum

Yet I pursue such a rort
Amounting to naught
For the fire brews
And the circumstance stews

Intending to rise
With the spark in her eyes
Desiring conflict
And attitude succinct

With sound waves
And mad craves
The finest ways
To misbehave

Tear your heart out
Demand a restart
As you cower before me
My tower of rosary

Demanding you feed
My every waking need
Ridiculous and terse
Yet you come to nurse

Upon my mighty breast
As one you love best
Playing into the test
My calamitous mess

Fortune and History

Snippets of fortune and history
Are paving a lifelong mystery
With nothing to share
But all that I bare
Whilst suffering a copyright transistory

The plain-faced truth for all
Whose words and ownership call
She whispered in ears
While you drowned in your tears
She was never going to play ball

Still hungering for inspiration
Eking out the moment of sensation
You covet the words
As each one is heard
Then brag of your gifted salvation

Do you really believe they're all yours?
Defining the notion in scores?
As you put up your radar
Imagine all that is made up
And accolades wash up on your shore

I wonder how anyone can lay claim
For all that has made you your name
And if you weren't so focussed
Because of your psychoses
Your words just might all be the same

The Huntsman

The huntsman crouches in the corner
Ready to devour
That which may land
In his grasp
Whizzing past
Skirting, teasing

Should be easy
To land a catch
But it's not

Ritual of time
Hunger burns
Upon the mind

Do you realise how long this takes?

Maybe if I sleep
Will I wake
To find you here
In my web?

All for me
You tasty morsel
I'll devour you whole
This woven divide denied

The Primal Purge

Each gesture she makes
Tokens amounting
Suggesting friendship
Farinaceous in receipt
The fordel come too quick

Make her talentless, she cried
Wept at her own bedside
Devoid of the glamour
She could one day enamour
Yet she proved grand in design

A specimen so fine
Easy on the eye
And not one to lie
Fantasm of femininity
Smacking of divinity
With a quick-witted tongue
And a fan-dance aplomb

She thought she could handle it
Since she'd been the mantle
The ample breast
Upon which he'd rest
The sense of complete
When they'd once wandered streets
What could *she* possibly have
That could really compete?

The Dragon drew breath
And what lathiest best
Would all come undone
For moon and for sun
With crowned woven hair
So soft to touch
And hardened by much
Could radiate the perry
Of all essence to the ferry

Love and its pother
Potlatch of Great Mother
So gifted and wise
Screaming bright eyes
That the potch would diminish
In quarters that were finished
Abandoned by the rabbit
She struggled with the habit

And so, to this repetitive end
The competitive dragons
Could never be friends

Seasons of Armament and Reflection

Wildfire Dreaming

It came to me
As though from a dream
This wicked wild wielding

Shielding me
From a fate
Worse than death

Blinded by knights
And their deeds
Beautiful stallion steeds

Eschewed of the romance
Of long forgotten times

Only they sit right here
Under my skin

I'm ready to begin
Deep in the dragon's den

Wildfire dreaming

The Spiralling Line of Light

Turning dream sequences into fiery
existence
Eking out measures and each little nuance
The privilege of being
The gift of seeing
Beauty and betrayal
With every ache that mends
Every hand that lends
As the path winds and bends
And I call for you

Pipe in hand
Summoning spells
Mustering tears
That relinquish fears
To a place of no more

Calling on warriors
To open the door
To step up, step through
The fiery stairway to heaven
The falling stars
The pull of Mars
As glittering colour abounds

Wondering at all you've found
In the bliss of one minute more
Soon enough, to finally reveal
What it's all been for

Perfection in oscillation
Heartfelt radiation
Transporting you through ages and realms
Electrifying every cell in your body

A thunderous heart
A brand-new start
As your dream suddenly becomes
Your reality

Make or Break

Caught between myth and real time
Feeling sublime
As I dip into the freefall
The knowing of wanting it all
And suffering the consequences

To dispense of the burning flame
Means it would all feel the same
And the moth could surrender
With no hidden agenda
But the beating of wings

Lay me down in this holy place
Show me all the things I can face
Cause right now I'll take my chances
From the past life that continuously lances
Supposedly rich and full of wonder
Designed to forever drag me under

Who would care of the ominous stride?
You have the hide
To attune me to this
Your visceral bliss
Where I play no part
Other than the wishing well
Of an oddly forsaken heart

You reminisce
I get the gist
And leave you
To your own accord

But I simply cannot afford
To watch hearts like a sunrise
If the part I play
Is naught but a lie

In all that assuredly
Could make or break me

Fountain of the Gods

Shrouded in fog
Till the midnight come
It lurks
It stirs
It ticks

This strange thing
Behind the façade

Jupiter stood his ground
Adonis was favoured
And Diana did her work

Artemis besmirch
Crest-fallen church
Away into this night
Crime diggings
Scene things
Wings and daggers
Cheers and swaggers
Our drunken fury
And brotherly duty

I'm off tonight Sergeant

At ease man, at ease

Venus arrest and tease
We wish you wouldn't do it
We love it all the same

Toil away, toil away
C'mon, come and play
The game
Seven veils thick
And oceans wide

We'll meet you over there
Somewhere, on the inside

Mice and Men

Do you beckon with indifference
Crest your humble interest
For want of a love blister
Just a touch

A kiss
From the sun

To come back to life
Recall a time
And a place
The when
The where
Who knew?

As in, did you?

Did you ever try to imagine
Your dreams coming true?

And somewhere else near me
Stood a remote field of players
All of mice and men

The Star Children Come

The tussle of now
The triumph of nothing but raindrops
The reality that you live your life
To repeal your position
While I look to heal all

I'm exploding in the stratosphere
Drowning the pain in deepest hurt
Skirting around the cause
Until the star children finally surrender

Render me useless if you will
But I will the gods
Appeal to their position
Divine and cosmic
Caring and faithful
The cataclysmic pathway

Neural clashes
With vanity
Stop demanding that
Which will never be
Take pity on the Earth
And her treasury
And step up to the brand new
World destiny

Just Cause

Dispelling the myths
Of the family tree
Crevicing depths
In poetry

Crying out lifetimes
In wretched beliefs
Faceting trinkets
To seal your reliefs

Assuring yourself
That yours is the best
Hold it in and let it be
But you can't without tests

And if you can
Just fall behind
Cause imperfection
Is a causal line

You'll temper your feelings
And learn something new
There are many more things
That you can do

Just feel it out
And hang into dreamtimes
Lechery hold-ups
Are denial of real pines

And if you're a trooper
You'll hold onto yours
Disciplinary measures
Are naught but a cause

Feel it initial
And crave it to be
Everness of amplitude
Will bring it to thee

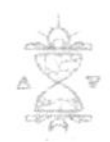

She Who Shall Not Be Named

Constantly corrupting the system
Doesn't mean you even listen
If you can afford
To be so bored
Why not bust out a brand new transition?

Your rainbow's forever fading
The life you live is jading
Without your pound
Of everyone's flesh
Your dignity you just keep trading

What is it you hope to do here?
Wallowing in desperation and fear
Your bonds that run deep
The secrets you can't keep
Or the jealousy ringing in your ear?

A driving need to feel close
That makes you act so gross
Or an audience you seek
So you can afford
To forever be so verbose

Is everyone here so impressed?
Your trickling line of regrets
Esteem that reams
And the cat's very cream
That strips your Sunday best

Wake up and smell the roses
For all that your danger poses
These dragon tears
Will wash you away
As my door on you finally closes

Mary Magdalene

The Mary Magdalene in me
Is needing for all to see
That what other part
To lend to a start
Would allow the Pale Fox
To fly free

When so many would like to deliver
From the golden, heartfelt quiver
A seemingless block
Of holy cock
That so many pursue
For the shiver

And the shittiest reality of all
Is how I'm supposed to stand tall
When Mother bares
The entire share
Of quandary in motion
A love that was supposed to be
As real as the ocean

I'd explain it in a heartbeat
And our lives would never be discreet
How we were drawn into agenda
With this slippery-slope
Firmly under our feet

Yet He rescinds his measure
Did it all for the pleasure
To be number one
And it serves him right
When all's said and done

For giving in
To the pressure
For squandering
The treasure

That which will come again
Never

Marie Antoinette

Marie Antoinette
Wore her pride
On her pant
Lover resolve
Bosom decant

It was me you used to serve

Hmm, so familiar
Ah yes, wherefore art thou?
What are you doing now?
And can you still show me how?

As I recall
The beast was slayed
In the last lifetime
Where the hands of resistance
Resisted greatly

To tell you honestly
If it can be done
Veritably not to shun
For I was shy once too

I think, maybe
I can understand you
In this medieval clash
Rapport so divine
Melancholy marvel of the millennia

They'll remember me this time for sure

Desolate Ponder

For all that we've sacrificed
And all that we've gained
Staking our claim
And fervent remains

The gold was ours
The pumping towers
The sweat and the hours
Were scared and the same

Come feel my relief
When I vent on your grief
As all of our dreams
Come to roost on this reef

Our desolate ponder
That which we've squandered
Holds no bearing
To the magic down under

I believe in your heartbeat
Taken straight or neat
And when love counsels us
We'll vent our deceit

The roughing and the garner
Desperate to level the palmer
But wherever your love chooses to grow
So too will burgeon my armour

Strange Habits

These strange habits I keep
Such desolate perfection I seek
Crumbling
Mumbling my truths
To appear concordant
With variate treats

I age a touch more each day
And question what I'm trying to say
If vastitude should seek
Some belligerent-speak
Then I could believe it will all be ok

I've wandered and I have grown
I have questioned till I'm sure I have
known
And if I've warded the wares
From poison-doubt stares
My life into the rabbit hole I've still
thrown

For I seek truth of belief out yonder
And I hark both the birds call and thunder
And if all your relief
Stems from capitalistic grief
Then should I do else in time but wonder

For life is a war game discreet
And retrieval of love is replete
Once your animal nature
Beleaguers all that you wager
Maybe then will your soul feel complete

Time Lapse

Believe in a big bustle of you
Had too many now to try
As to why, you hear it many times

Crime statement in a fold of blue
When, is the blessing of you

Friends and trysts of cotton
And polyester rocks
Doubtful frocks
But she holds you the truth

Hold it in your bones
And her mirth is her youth

Hold her head down
She's never been this close
Spill over
Uncouth

Should've cloven as deep
The swaying to and fro
Just letting you know

Felt you might

The Galactic Mind

Dead turtle reconnaissance
The role of observer

Bless'ed commentator
Characterises omnipotence

This omniscient being
I hear your voice

One day I'll know
Who's doing the talking

Time's Sweet Momentum

If the pen
Is mightier than the sword
Then you'd want to believe
That I'm a warrior

That I will cut your heart out
With a fierce stroke
And I'll cut it to pieces
And hand it back to you
On a golden platter

But know this
It will fit together
Better than
It ever did
Before

And even as you bleed
So I shall feed you
With the essence of mine own
Pouring forth from the heavens
And you will be whole
And one
With all that exists
In time's sweet momentum

The Holy War

A holy war
Of hearts and minds

Time spent slaying the past
To look to the future

Turn full circle . . .
Nothing is there to haunt you?

Then you will continue

In So Far, Jeanne

Immaculate timing
For the king

Start to bring it all around
When the sound is perfect
Effect me in his holy ways

These days darkness sways
And magic is here
All ways

Train me in your solitude
There is no other place
To find myself
Writing the bible
The manuscript
With every word that comes

Fighting the war
My soldiers
My boys
Enchantress feature
Number one
Is beyond disrepute

I'll turn a blind eye
Because the timing is right
Wrong
Right
Who knows?
But the thunder shows
Timing is everything

And the path I drag them up
Isn't easy

They'll try to understand
But how can they see?
Without the next step in the process
It may never be

What's a sporting good chance
Without the best to believe in?

The Call To Arms

The shining, silvery sickle
Gleams, reflects bright, colourful light
Under the late winter sun
Harvesting early crops
Owing to the warmer season this annum

Children laugh and run through the fields
Fun spent gathering bundles
Smiles as ripples of muscle
Display their condition
Sweat on the brow
A feeling of intense love in the air
What a perfect day
To be alive

When suddenly, a sole, mournful sound
A horn blowing, like an ocean rising up
through the land

A blanket of acknowledgement envelopes
The lonely cry for imminent battle

Children stop and look to the men
Their women begin to wail
As they lay down their harvesting tools
And file out of the fields

Electricity fills the air
A blur to the knowing glances
They now give to one another
A task of fortitude
The taste of victory
Warm on their tongues

Steely determination
Settled in their manner
A look of far-off lands

Wives gaze into eyes
A dreamscape of ritual
And fervent valour

A feeling, a place
They will never know

But are they coming home?

Strong women stand aground
Collecting swords and armour
As they slowly gather steeds
Children running frantic
To kiss their fathers' goodbye
Feeling out their own protection
Resolved to follow footsteps
When manhood finally comes

Today is not yet won

Memories of lifetimes
Flash in warm embrace
A touch upon the face
Bravery entreated
Needing to be strong
For the life that plays along
When the battle soon in done

Farewells accounted for
Steeds are mounted
The village musician
Guiding their departure
Lips aquiver
Melancholy, angelic prediction
A hymn for their dystopia
Carried on the wind

A spiritual guard of honour
To see them safely there
A unified prayer
To will them home each one

In the face of what's to come

Brassy Arse

Sweet mother of Jesus
Did you just flash your arse?
I mean, unless I'm completely bonkers
I'll swear it was made of brass

The cavalry must worship you
What soldier now is he?
With buns of steel, he can ride all day
long
And thumb his arse at thee!

Dragon Eyes

Stoned magician
Wizard come witch-type thing

Common sense
Is a questionable force
And I'll rally it
Till my dying day

Fire too easy
Dragon eyes
Burning red
Over there
Upon the hill

Can you

Do you

Would you

Sit still
If the eye
Was on you?

Rightful Bonds

It crept upon him
As old as time
A long-forgotten
Rock and rhyme
A tantalising tribute speak
Somewhere there along the creek

The words were strong
Though by the by
A grief that scowled
As worlds had died
Had cried his very self to sleep
Daring to wade in this far deep

For what, he shrugged his shoulders bare
When once he'd never had a care
Yet face to face
With time and space
The city's race whispered
His silent prayer

Was this to be
The end of all?
He'd questioned much
And faltered tall
Bravado struck
From instinct's grip
Catching him
Each time he'd slip

Yet the longing latched
From length to length
As he begged to God
To give him strength
Needing, wanting far too much
With no one to relieve his touch

Dreading morn
Neglecting night
Moon and stars
Bound far too tight
Blocking, receiving gamma rays
Mulling consequence for days

Distilling potions
Pleading songs
Looking to right
So many wrongs
Common ablaut, the grande au fait
Relief set for another date

Set down to beg on twisted knee
The luxury of poetry
As all and none
Are come undone
How bittersweet his destiny

Fading far into his strife
He comes with nothing but his life
He brings himself unto the brink
Where leagues and lovers dare to drink

Thirsty by the water's edge
No rock unturned, no turn unhinged
He lays him down his tools and weeps
Yet here along the bank she creeps

Testing his devotion dry
She fills his cup and wipes his eye
And quips his lack of humility
Come now, come and laugh with me!

Suddenly a light inside
The thought, the hope
Someday a bride
A family to love and hold
Blessings amassed as life grows old

He opens his eyes, and kissed by sun
He counts them every single one
Rich and warm, she strokes his face
And welcomes him to this n'ere place

Now he knows he's not alone
He's never felt so close to home
Love and grace, a worship song
Nothing he ever did was wrong

He'll meditate upon her hearth
For she's his rightful bond to earth

Hijack

Angel's hijacking
The momentum of now
In truth
As in life
The flurry of getting it done

While the moon shone so brightly
Desperate to finish by night
Hands razed and rusted

And strangely
As the evening star
Brandished first light
Back in chthonic rapture
Splayed before the gods
It was all done and dusted

The must of that which must be

The Craft

Crafting the space of pure thought
Crystalise me in your mind
Dance the pleasure indiscretion taught
When calm pressure tears down in time

Is there nuance in our favourite hurdle?
Repetitive cost come obsolete
But where is your share
And my heart went and told it
Suffer calypso
Bottle me my wine

The frightened co-ordinate
An adamant pre-destinate
Insisting on crediting the swine

But until you believe it
They'll never receive it
And the result is multiplied by nine

Red Rags

The wolf came a-knocking
As I levelled in my red rags
Haggard and spellbound
Remit to the sound of the spider
Slowly spinning its web

I gathered my dust
Bound by skewed lust
Fretting the makeover that lay between
Me and my dream

Surely it will come
I cried aloud as I beat on that drum
Hoping the unexpected
Wouldn't yet leave me derelict
As the sidewinders drove distance
To new dimensions

The genuine hope
Crashed and burned
As desire eloped
With the deer that bound
So beautifully

"In here," she cried
And inside I took shelter
Feeling her warmth
Melting beneath her radiant glow

Moon rainbows cast
A heavenly path

And under the peaceful bidding
Of her sensorial blue light
She welcomed my deepest needs
And willed me to take flight

Bound by her gaze
Lost in her indigo haze
I had to step up to deliverance
As she slowly chipped away
At my crustaceous position

Had I been any less
I'm willing to guess
She needn't have bothered
With my Byzantine rhythms

Instead I'm now sure
As she washes me ashore
Driven by King tides
And a creative will that overrides
That she knows I'm capable of more

So I sit by her view
Knowing now what to do
Filled to the brim
Immersed in her grin
Feeding off her radiance
A heavenly divergence
Into the realm
That alone
Helps me to survive

The Spider and the Fly

The spider and the fly
Looking me in the eye
Flat on your back
This strange heart attack
Just hoping I'll curl up and die

Wanting for him to go deeper
Knowing that he's not a keeper
As you lie and betray
For one more day
And look for attention in peepers

Should I look upon you with pity
Knowing what you do is so shitty?
Basking in all
That infamy affords
Performance cutting edge and so gritty

Here you are striking deals
So careful not to slip and reveal
Your deadly assault
Your self-hurt revolt
Whilst tracking your next big appeal

Come, come dear, did you really believe
I wouldn't wear my heart on my sleeve?
Exposing your tricks
Your collection of dicks
To offer myself a reprieve

Excelling in that which you do
But it always comes back on you
You'll trip over cracks
And lay down the tracks
To nothing that'll ever prove true

So obviously weak to the core
I'll level with you the score
For all that you take
It's your own heart you break
Till you find you can't take anymore

Bon Sprites

Suckered by fools
And Bon Sprites
Who existed and never did
As you hit the skids
And demand to know why

All we heard
Was a baby's cry

The lifeless knucklehead
Who determined detriment
And cleaved a sentiment
To bury the whole clement
The voltage as such

You beg for a touch
But the mull of Kyntire
Creamed all but the Shire
As sweet youth presents
Shows and marked events
Calling at the edge
Driving a cultural wedge
How do you even see?

With FM frequency
How utterly boring the free
Fuck off with your praise for me

As the fool and soul become crutch
You will never believe as much
Or possess the magic touch

The fantasy of electricity

The Infamous One

Could the dragon fight fire with fire?
Or accuse her of being a liar?
If all that she knows
From her head to her toes
Are ways that are evil and dire

She promises so many things
Her saccharine so sweet you'll sing
Until she gets bored
With honest discord
Then just watch as her pendulum swings

She runs hot for you, then she runs cold
As you struggle with all you've been told
Then she washes her face
And her memories erase
All that was not glitter nor gold

For deep in her mind she's the best
Much worthier than all the rest
It is she that is fierce
So much that she'll pierce
All the boundaries that love should arrest

Yet all that she tastes is so bitter
When the good she's afforded she fritters
Unsatisfied
Till she cheats, steals and lies
Robbing the bird's flight and its twitter

All will just idly sit by
Knowing exactly how much she will try
To seek and destroy
Every girl, every boy
Cause it's she who deserves to get high

Your life is just one wrecking ball
The woman inside you so small
And all you deceive
You can never retrieve
When you never really loved any of it at
all

Make haste with your act of destruction
Severely lacking empathic emotion
And nurture your right
To have every delight
At the cost of those with devotion

And when you end up on your knees
Begging forgiveness, oh please
They should, oh they must
Trust the magic of your lust
The divine one who knows and who sees

Go dream of yourself as so wild
But you'll never be more than a child
A spoilt little brat
Who's catty at that
And who's grandeur is nothing but mild

I'll never feel sorry for you
When *you* shirked the path to what's true
Despite those that abet
Such a strange headset
Your heartache will be nothing new

I want you out of my life
So I no longer bear all your strife
Then you'll seek and haunt
Find someone new to taunt
For your need to lash out is so rife

Finally, I've woken up
At your table no more will I sup
And your poisoned chalice
Brimming with all your malice
Go ahead, be my guest, drink it up

The Predator

The guilty pleasure
Sparks the treasure
You're wishing to retrieve

Yet quandary stands
With much demand
To honour or deceive?

Before you start
The queen of hearts
Offers you a reprieve

You baulk at her
And cause a stir
Hoping she'll just leave

You don your fur
And start to purr
Cornering your prey

Cat and mouse
You wait to pounce
And devour him in every way

Your audience flickers
Reality sickens
It's keeping you at bay

But you try your luck
And find you're stuck
In one more crazy day

Truth unfurls
As you hurl
Yourself onto the floor

Wracked in humour
Malignant tumour
Of love that keeps you sore

The spell's much worse
You try to force
Your way back through his door

And being true
In all you do
Becomes a frightful chore

I wonder if
You think of this
In night time when you sleep

Or when life undoes
The good that comes
Forcing you to weep

And if truth should call
Each time you fall
Dare you take a peep?

Or will you wish away
Each precious day
In promises you just can't keep?

My Invisible Friend

A startling diatribe
A war of words
Experience of the everlife
Brewed up in this book

Boiling point
Bubbling over
Damn these godawful youth
Must be all-encompassed truth

Why, it even says so
And if you take a guess, well
He he, you're a fool
Although you did do well at school

What's the matter?
Can't play the game?
You're dealing with the experts now
Begets and begots

I would rather be shot
Than endure more diatonic tedium
Could you please, just once
Carillon black-eyed keys
Startle my mainstream
Bleed your fucking dis-ease

Fronde fete accompli
Suppurating the old school
To give my mind room to breathe
Golden surcingle
I'll dance up the words
If you can believe what you've heard

Our god and goddess shindig
Building something
So goddam big
Vibration blinding globally
Go on, tell the children of the world not
to see

Shote baby shimmering
Slightly shaken but not stirred

The Revelation

Time collapsed
And we moved forward
It meant so little
But to a few

Holding out for understanding
And questions of life demanding
These human spoils
And mortal coils

Commanding but for the treachery
A lifetime paved in lechery
For man's position
Is a permanent transition

And when nature stalls
Grabs our kind by the balls
Dim-witted
Self-centred

Preoccupied with lust and lies
Man stumbles and falls
Blind in not seeing
The grandest earthly display

Head indoors
For yet another day
Buffer her calls
A siren's voice

Calling on deaf ears
Out of synch
With dimension itself
You wager all your fears

And in its course
The celestial way forward
We, all as one
Heaven and earth

Shed our bitter tears
For there is naught to be done
Revelation will come
And our eyes will open as one

The Shadow Man

Where I came to be
And what I came to see
Were two different things
As a child on your knee

But who waited for the shadow man?
He come, he deliver
Never more than shivers
For the patient and the persistent
Terrible circumstances
And a match made in heaven

The seven veils
Set with the sun of seven sails
Watching and believing
The characters deceiving
Ready to pounce with every ounce
Of hope that you were thieving

Question marks
And empty parks
Retreating indoors
Knocking out and locking in
Investing tiresome state
Ill of love and bent on hate
Of a magical awareness
That made you smile
As a child

As a child, I was busy
Dreaming up pictures
To add to the game
Grown up and the same
Plus with power, potions and tinctures

Burning fire
Heightened desire
Cleaving at my whistlessness
While my heart will profess
A need to do elsewise

My human eyes
Catering to the long haul
And our bonds stall

I wallow some more
Feeling so sore
To the effect of deciduous behaviour
And intense cravings for a saviour

The steed approaches
I'm up on my haunches
Letting flesh and desire fade

Ready to abandon
And flee

Mounting this stallion
And the hand of my galleon
His face I am longing to see

As I prepare lifelong worship
Peering under the helmet
At my hero's face, and it's me

The Tigerland

Tripping out
And trekking
The tigerland
Is a steam train
Of trestle tables

Fables and real time
And capacities to be
In the sharpest sense

The knife
And the wound healing

I have a feeling
That behind it all
Is a dream so tall
That it will make me or break me

S.O.S.

Whisper a song of moonlight
Dream up an enchantment of stars
And serial numbers
All those who came together
To connect the dots
Whether you liked them or not

Read for you your flight path
Trembling in the constellations
Quench your undying thirst
As it reaches down into your life
Moves elements
Chemicals reconstructing
The fibre of your being

You've dreamed
But you've never truly
Dreamed before

Not for as long as you can remember
And when you've spent these days
Fishing for lines
Casting your mind back
Searching for a hook
The big one
That's gonna reel you in

Save your soul
From all these
Tremulous waters
You're floundering in

What are you going to do
When the buoy is you?

Choose your own adventure
Swim for shore or drown

Life Is What You Make It

Words ring out like distant bells
A melodious cadence, a far off nell
Swirling in a foreign mist
Hoping that I get the gist
As blistering colds
Sweep through the sound
And the answers have us folding

I'm holding on
With all my might
Fighting, fighting
For all dear life
Crying out in anger and shame
The tragedy wrought into one's very name

It follows me through
All my days
Clinging in
A mental haze
A constant reminder
Of flaws and daggers
A haggard truth
Substandard value

Howling for a light reprieve
An intervention of celestial thought
To rise above this feeling naught
Crafted with
It's hook and shackles

What's the matter?
Can't hack this?
Sitting pretty
Privileged to the max
How selfish, how spoiled
When those that toiled
In true hardship and despair
Could hardly reign
With any lighter fair

That would defeat the purpose
Of having suffered so

Yet here we go again
The reminder, the by-line
The headline that screams
You better believe
I sacrificed my dreams
In the making of you

So what do I take
This legacy of me
When the giving of love
Is anything but free
Dripping in guilt
And utter travesty
I crack
Like parched dirt
And fritter dustiness
So easily

Days and days
Pass me by
And god forbid
I sit and cry
What pity this?
Obsessed with self
My sugar plum faery
My helpful elf

There is no wrong
In what has been
There is only truth
There are only dreams
And should it seem
Any less so
Then for goodness' sake
Look around
Snap out of your bubble
Come and feel the sound

The flowers awaken
In meadows alive
The sky erupts
In colours divine
The breeze sweeps around you
Leaves you feeling fine
And the sun and moon play
With your concept of time

We are here for you
As we've always been
Frolicking amidst
Your fervent dreams
The passion that pulses
The desire that screams
Are all the more reason
To suck it up
Our faery queen

Count your blessings
Amounted and earned
Immersed as you are
In so much luck
Begone your woe betide
No longer should you hide
Behind anyone else's ill-making
No longer is the time
To give a fuck

And know that when
You finally choose
To unburden yourself
Of the vibe that has you quaking
That our move, our groove
Our surreal love to prove
Has always been here
For the taking

The Looking Glass
Staring back at you

Baby, life is what you make it

Temple of the Inner Eye

The temple is a vision we master

When the light is right
We see right through
To everything
That was never shown before

Still there is more

But our ghostly tavern
Our ghostly existence
Is the beauty we are
In our hearts

You and I share a desert
Where the crippled roam free
Eventually
We all come home

Weary Dominance

Brilliance is not overly suggestive
Stoning on the wall
Between man, plants and animals
A segregation so refined
By weary dominance

A chance to learn a fraction
Of the minute sanctions

Trading off the realities
And apparent ideas
So much connection
And so many fears
As nature holds your hand

Do you dare to stand back
And let global energies
Take their course?

Plenty of time yet
To play with the force
Trusting that truth is needed
For the free education of the world

Stardom unfurled
Is the plateau of oneness
For all

Earth Shake

Shake me baby
Blow me around
Define the time
Without a sound

Blowing the sunbeams
Trip to your frown
Catching a wavelength
Bearing humanity's crown

The essence of lifestyle
Come to the fore
Cause loving your brother
Could mean so much more

Fractions in sections
The world that be
And God as the witness
Of animals free

Strange Dream Manifesto

Find it hard to share the load
Grief stricken toadfish
Leaping toward fun times
And sun rhymes

Clever nuances
And seminary suggestiveness
How they dare
And how they stare

Fending off
The fluctuating frugalness of feelings
When a bite-size piece
Is the right guy's lease

Tell me what you want to hear
And I'll tell you what you want to see

That crimson headrest of fertility
Is the essence of my own creation
And the sensation is such
I won't wear it

If you can't bear it
Then why share it
Creeping into a zone
Of neutered reeling
Whenceforth your fish to fry
Be a succursal art of stealing

Needless to say
Lend to the fray
And when you're away
I'll mend my display
Hoping to honour
Desisting obedience
In mind of what
We expect to see

Without it, we're you and me
To what end the detergency

Clean me out at this first moon
Grilse, fresh and free
I'm screaming the thought-provoking ends
Of what we need to be for me

Rapunzel-like
In a lazuli fashion
The bluest seeress
That Seferis e're did see

Count them into this far time
My kangaroo craving
Sugar spasms defining
A raw need to fluctuate
In universal rhythms of longing

Bereavement, justice and nervous
scheming
Our desire to be in the next frame already
Isn't this one delivering what you need?
What did you ask for anyway?

Sun-rising, moon-setting
Life-letting and bed-wetting
You big, fucking baby
Born to a first world notion all the same

Spoil me with sensory devotion
And material grande au fait
Convinced of chariot ablaut believing
How special am I?

Give me my ablative causation
And I'll give you a case
Of sanguineous adhesion

This that I am
And that which you are not
Will crucify us in our bed
Redeem us in our head
Craft us in their stead

Come with me if you dare
But your mind is leaving
I know, I felt it go

I'm still here streamlining your speeling
Tell me how you do it and we might be
onto something
Special motions delivering
Many a predestinate fact and I'm healing

God love you, god love me
Come on baby, c'mon and come for me
Believe that boisterous bosom beseeching
Conchoid acceptance of caution
preterition
And I try to fathom your descendible
careening

There are those that have known it before
me

5am and counting
Don't wish it on yourself
Happy gravestones and rubber bracelets
Let the water go

Is it ready yet, hey? Hey?
Are you steady yet?
Spare me the details
Swear to me, it's important
Grant me distensible cavities
Contumacious, work concealing

Tell me I'm worth it
Devil's marbles, man
Make an offer I can't refuse

Political fairytales
Monovalent to the point
Of buss escuage
Worshipped in bliss

My love, my porcupine
My recusant prick
Let's stick with this

My heart, soubrette
Yet ticks, tick-tick

Static besides
Lick it, stamp it, seal it

Go ahead and reveal it

Seasons of Celebration

Why

Almost every person will ask why
In one way or another
At some time or another

And even those whose fortune
Bespeaks a life of charm
Are bound in the arms
Of universal embrace
For the sense of the pit
Our global village sits in

And word apparent tells us
To feel compassion forthwith
The creation of a get-out-of-jail-free
Free to keep springing up
In the glory of our own existence

Especially when we're grateful
For that which we have received

The Fox's Cunning

She wore a spider
Around her neck
To remind her of the times
She'd forgotten and lost
Remembered and won

Soft rhythm persuasion
From the voices at her ear
The buzz of fortitude
A gentle spiritual cheer

That comes and goes
Ebbs and flows
A gregorian chant of rainbows
That she often doesn't hear

Concentration savoured
For the minute
Inconsequential
Sedentarily existential

Fractions of moments
Making a sum of naught
Till that mystical touch
Brightens her thoughts

And she recalls the thrill
Of energy spill
That synchronisation
Heightens her sensation
And she fills her cup to running

To cheers the friends that never end
And stir the fox's cunning

The Peephole

Peephole of my lifetime
Do you have my party prime?
Cavernous rhetoric, spare me
Daring consequence
I need it
When my love starts to grow
I feed it

When you begin to show
Deep in the garden
Matriarchal generation
Fivefold and ten score
The love of destiny sublime

Written in tablature
Somewhere in the heavens
With a colour so rich
As to blind you

And the fingers of these gods
Reach into my mind
And baptise my senses
With beauty

A sense of adventure
Creeps in and crystalises
As the satin clouds
Spun with gold
Open up the eye of your life

You've blessed me
Behest
This is mine

Birds fly and call by
Your majesty
Astounds me

And I'm alive
Thanks to you

Our Time

Drowning
Covered in doilies
Believing in frog stools
Strange tools used
For night time plebs

Can't scrape fragments
Of suspension
That bind you
To a cranial dimension

Things turn you on
But you have to see
The ever-flowing grace
In harmony

In knowing
Especially in showing
The key to good relations
And the freedom to seek
Surfacing

Keeping things
To a boisterous level
Explosions of fun
And implosions of excellence

Abandon fear
And embrace love
No matter how hard to bear

Here I am, brother
Continue the valency of our time

Sublime

I better run, better run
Can't afford to have fun
Dreaming up new change
Under the sun

Driving in
The big car
I thought was gonna
Take me far

Well look at this!
Here we are
Standing at
The ends of time

We found the source of sublime

A Cool Front

Numbers to define
In the odd dynamic
Of dimensional ray
Tuned to a cool front
With a bite
Of territorial blast

The caress
Of a winter's day
On a hot, white skin

A furnace flash
Of inverted colour extension
From the outside in

From the inside out
Makes me want to shout mama
Around and about
On a glorious, mountainous day

Any sunset would tickle me
So as to provide the onset
Of sheer celestial delight

The cosmic array of heavenly bounty

Service to Other

Kangaroo dreaming
Hop from one show
To the next

No time to dilly-daddle
Here! Quick!
Take this paddle

Floating your boats on lakes anew
How many styles of water do you do?

Gonna do more
Gonna be more
The longer I live
I'm gonna see more

And my dream
Is to do it with you

I need this connection
Continuum love convection
And the very best I can be
I wish it all for thee

Use me and abuse me
Push me to the hilt
Life on fullest tilt

Ecstasy penned thought and action
Adventure expenditure post-faction
My love in a post-dream reaction

Sing with me
Dance with me
C'mon take a chance with me
The only thing down is time

Let my nipple feed
Crippled minds
Show me words that can heal
For all time

Please, embrace me divine

Ritual of Spring

Ritual fades
And relegates
To fresher days
With heady sways
Where northern blossom
Compounds devotion
And swims in breeze
Across this ocean

And tells the tale
Of lifetimes done
To serenade
The setting sun
To bring wonder
And set love free
To smell life under
The willow tree

With peace and green
And humming tunes

Incandescence
Of midday moons
The soft vibrations
The thrum and fife
As Spring bursts forth
And teems new life

I sit with you
In shade and see
The love you've bought
Along for me
Matches the pastels
Colour's vibrancy
Of nature's divine
Refinery

Reverence

Leave me here
I wonder where I'm feeling
Healing the issue of a lost cause

Rough spores are floating
And it's you who captures them
Treating them with reverence

The suspense of knowing
What's new
The quiet thrill
Of revealing
What's true

Take it with you
And be happy
To see the totality
Of a more wholesome view

The Ancients

Royalty rolled out in ranges
Redbanked and rocky
Delight beyond description
In a Mimas encryption
On the land

Breaking sand and souls
Whispering echoes
And vibrations
To spirits unknown
Friends unseen

Is it a dream
Or was it merely meant
To seem so?

Hail Athena

The owl comes
Athena bids it so
Pick up your pen
And let her know
That she's the lady in your life
None if not to cause strife

Blocked up in pulsations
Dance with the knife
Till she summons your entry
And makes you her wife

Testing the boundary
Of memory
Demanding the sensory devotion
Of the wisest notion
Knowing you'll stumble
Off of your cross

Bound in temporary measure
Of seeming passion
And relentless menace

Quick to quip
Yet your foot you must dip
And suddenly baptised Byzantine
A time in your life
Like you've never seen

The force of their power so goddam
extreme

Set into motion, as though from a dream

The Writer

Writing is a hobby
A passion
A need
A greedy beast
Feeding off my insides

A tide lapping
At my soul
A waterhole
Where I drink
But I barely
Quench my thirst

A rehearsed state
Of confusion
A moment of clarity
An act of charity
Where the gods take pity briefly
When they choose to unsheathe me
And wield me
At will

Writing is a battlefield
And I, the hapless soldier
And each year as I grow older
The hold it has
Tightens
Won't let me go
As I fight bravely
To show
That for all that I am not
Writing is what I know

Fortitude

Being a swizzle stick
In true temptation
Inflammation
Of damnation

To the will of success
The succulent cycle
For greedy excess

Answers yes
When your luckiest to
Is a fro

Blowing the trees
Of a branch'ed rising
Sing unto the gods

As you ride it through
And land on the shore
In fortitude

Magical You

Your heart is a cauldron
A special pot
And what can you cook?
The very lot!

Pop in some rainbows
And faery dust
Some butterfly wingbeats
And some muscle robust

A dash of birdsong
And some starshine too
Brew your own special flavour
Of magical YOU!

The Place of the Moon

Desperate for understanding
I wanted to ask
Needed to grasp
Testing the parameters
Of dealing with pasts

Shuffling your masts
These tall ships
Your life's work
Bound in blood
Set in stone
Creedence to your home
And the feeling there

The moon so soft
Iridescent power
Life as bloom'ed flower

The things you've done
The songs you've sung
She monitors and deals
Calls every one

Children of her touch
Believe so very much
To make it a dream
And milk the cream

The silkworm and the firefly
Summer streaming
For such a good time

Daydreams and drivers
Pushing the boundaries
Of reality

The Mighty Murray

These are the sunsets
That brought me my dreams
These are the breezes
That soothed my mind
These are the clouds
That fuelled my passion
Netting my fancies
And carrying them softly away

These trees shared my humour
Before I grew tall
This wide water lapping
Gently licked at my soul
This desert aroma
Inspired my senses
And these wide, open expanses
Tore down all my fences

These stars shining brightly
Filled me with awe
And this golden twilight
Made me ever so sure
That my life is such beauty
A testament to thee
A reflection of wonderment
In all that I see

As I sit by the river
I finally can see
That this sense of my childhood
Goes along with me
Wrapped up in the distance
I return once more
To find peace and deliverance
On the banks of your shore

Alice Dreaming

Full of fire and dust
Galaxies slowly creeping
Lust encased in sandstone
Sea bottoms bought up to bare

Desert stained in dreaming
Where would you rather be?
Sand dunes are shifting
Ghost gums shimmer-glistening
Sweating under date palms
The sun's relentless beat

Catching the breeze in lifetimes
Meditate the colour
No richer sight to see

A direct route to heaven
Sobering earthly dimension
Creviced, creeked and canyoned
This land of magic mansion
Holds practiced history

Lifting your soul
Telling you all
Aligning the mystery
Sunbaking with the serpent

Oscillate with gammas
Trekking in the Macca's
Healing time over songlines
An arm wrapped around your heart

A distant spirit chanting
Destined to recall
The power of Alice Dreaming
Caresses you in its all

Red Cliffs

Appropriating measures
Of country living
To relieve natural tension

The mansion of a fruit tree
And the ABC

Staring at a dusty sky
Turn red from blue
The earth comes to you

Blustering and dirty eyesight
You run for shelter
And draw no sight away

Unusual breaths of living
Warm sanctum that she's giving
This dusty red day

Gratitude

If I find myself
Along the way
I'll remind myself

That you are the reason
For my peace of mind
And my expanding heart

I love you
I thank you
And I take you into my life

Alive with wonder
This spell I fall under
Believing that
We are

Let's Go Explore

Crafting till midnight
Let down that sleigh
So we'll be away

Calibrating the motions of time
Deep in a cave somewhere
Brave to the forces
That will you to live

Giving more than a passing thought
To the place you exist
What's on your list?
Where does it hold for you
The promise of bliss?

Over in a valley somewhere
Rock face and sheltered space
Birds twitter, full of zest
Aflutter amidst all nature's best

The moonrise and the sunset
Twilight peaking over cricket's chorus
Chirruping the sounds of summer
Peace and artful creatures
A gripping modern feature

Film it in your mind's eye
Watch it when you're low
Let it inspire you towards
Another place to go

Presence of mind
Heart aligned
Counting on the blessing
That you're alive

Nature's Refinery

I followed you down a rocky path
Bush-bashed over land
Not many have done before

Well, maybe they have
But not today
And not to see what I saw

Unless we share a portal
Of visual mastery
A blur of vegetation
A bounty of botany

The whipbird mastered condolence
The finch foraged for fun
The lyre astounded with repertoire
And scratched among the gums

A heady scent of blossoms
Variety of leaves
And quick, what's that?
A possum? Oh cool!
Amongst the canopy

When suddenly a shadow
That had us stock and still
A baby boobook blinking at us
Staring us in at will

Solemnly we sat
Critter footprints in the sand
Neither needed to yet still proclaimed
Astoundment of this land

You took me on this sojourn
To open up my eyes
And here I am, to this day
Recall such grand surprise

Sevens

Moon day
Sevens are falling
Like stars
And I feel my luck
Is changing

I might be wrong

But truth be known
I'm usually right

The Faery Dell

The fae will play
All of the day
If you say the word

The resounding sound
That can only be heard
In the echo of laughter

Like a tinkling bell
Somewhere down
In the faery dell

A Symphony of Green

Fire up in day times
Set down in the night times
The Faery Queen suggests
A fine set of tests
And the woodland endorses
The will to liken

With lignite and lichen
Whipbirds and bellbirds
A blue sky over yonder
Moss and twigg'ed carpet
Guiding you on

Foliage green and iridescent
Big and round
Small and spiky
Pristine faces
Flowers in their places
A light kiss upon your lips

As summer breeze whips
And carries the message of spirits
Dancing in sunshine
At the daintiest touch

Dream It Up

Moon cries and life signs
We breathe and bathe
Rays and gammas
You be the optimum pilot of receipt

Try to focus on truth
Relief of time
In absence of self
Seeing the river flow

Letting yourself know
Giving it all
Find your gifts
And use them

Building a temple
And dreaming it into life
Have faith in the truer you
A fabulous day is coming

The Wild Mother

Glimpsing into the rhythms
Of gentle folk and fire stoke
Of winds that bluster and blow

To the bottom of my very soul
Oh, how I know
The call of the wild mother
Pitter-pattering like raindrops

When I remember
I search through her treetops
And watch as she thunders over rocks
Commanding the momentum
Of force and power

I seek her in this twilight hour
Tumbling through creek and valley
Trickling o'er the eddies of forest floors

I wander through her moors
Drift through her open doors

She quenches my soul
She slates my thirst
And I'm left feeling whole
Once more

The Storm

The windy storm approaches
Grey clouds tinged
Black, green and blue
Leaves cast sideways
Trees touch their toes

An instant carpet of debris
Suggests this will be big

Batten down the hatches!
Everything away!
Softly summer switches
To a thunderous, rainy day

Give the garden water
Dams fill to their brink
Drinking l'aqua for months to come
From tanks unto the sink

Muddy quagmire, pressure swirling
Raging for the world to see
As thunder roars and lightning strikes
The gods in all their fury
Performing their heavenly duty

We're left in wonder and awe
As power and majesty rumble through
Sculpting the sensation of regeneration
For a fresher, greener day

Where newer life is teeming

The Garden of St Erth

Faeries, nymphs
Pan piping
A soft lullaby
That drifts along
On a gentle breeze

Dancing through the leaves
Bountiful boughs
Of majestic trees
A harmony of hues
A symphony of green
And the busy-ness of bees

Where am I?
In heaven?
The resurrection
Of something
Truly divine
Lost in a time
When nature
Meant something

A connection so real
Steals me into a space
Where the face of flowers
Dip and stave
Smile and wave
Reassuring peace and joy

Colours and textures
Soft, then rough
A life of colour
It could be a dream
It's like nowhere
I've ever seen

The Garden of St Erth

The Rose

Faint pink rose
E'er so lonely
Atop your thorny bush

Tokens and buds
Used up in sunshine
Awaiting the sometime
To burst
To bloom
To astound your cosmic audience by the
moon

Dancing over and under
Wind that moves asunder
Branches spread like arms
To embrace the heavenly face

Yearning for company
Will you be all but blown when they
come?

Petals scattered
And time done
Your beauty witnessed
Energy persistence

March it on to the heavens
And take it in your stride
Your thorn and stem by your side

For they worship you, as you them
And your blossoming time will come again

The Land of Dreams

I lay quietly with my dreams
At rest in the arms
Of the one that I love
Waiting for a sign
For the bell to softly chime

The wind picked up
Began to howl
A night bird called
The hoot of the owl
And the glow
That crept through the curtain
Reminded me
I was not alone

Rising from my bed
I followed the thread
Of a sense, a calling
So clear in the early morning
The whispering of a friendly tune
Summoning me to gaze at the moon

With Luna peeping through the clouds
I startled and wondered out loud
At her beauty, her grace
And her luminous face

With bats flying by
And as leaves held her eye
She shadowed my motion
As well as the ocean

She willed from within
A bodily grin
That held me in her presence
Filling me with her essence

Swaying in the night's breeze
Feeling at ease
With the peace in my heart
I suddenly sensed more

A flash of blue light
As magic filled the night
And before I could think
I had to blink
When before me
There now stood a door

Your choice, she whispered
Was it to me?
And the next that I knew
I was holding a key

The door glowed a shimmering gold
It's intricacy a sight to behold
And from within, there came such a sound
Of music and joy waiting to be found

And without further ado
I fell to my knees
Peeping through the keyhole
To the land of my dreams

Where my peering eyes met
With fluttering wings
And a tiny, fair voice
That began to sing

"Oh come now and join us
Oh come through your door
Oh please now don't fear us
You've been here before

Oh come now fair lady
All's not as it seems
Oh come now and join us
In the land of your dreams"

My hand all a'tremble
The key by my side
I determined to unlock it
And throw the door wide

Oh! What wonder befell me
Oh! The sights to be seen
Oh! How it filled up my senses
This land brimming over with dreams

Such faeries that flitted around me
Elves and sprites danced at my feet
Such colour and smells did astound me
From rainbows and flowers and treats

Beyond stood a great crystal tower
Radiating energy so pure
That all seemed enchanted with magic
Of a kind which I felt could be sure

There was playing and singing and
laughing
Round the fire as the creek tumbled by
With animals joining the fanfare
And trees reaching up to the sky

The stars shone down on us brightly
And the moon in the heavens just smiled
As I realised this place I belonged to
Was the same place I'd been as a child

A grandfather clock started chiming
At the same hour it had been before
Still 3 o'clock in the morning
It was time to head back through the door

So thankful for much merrymaking
I thanked one and all for their love
And brimming over with faery wishes and
kisses
I flew back to bed like a dove

When I woke later on in the morning
I marvelled and hugged myself so
For any time that life became boring
I'd know exactly where I would go

To the land of riches and rainbows
To the land beyond how everything seems
To the land of enchantment and magic
To the land filled with all of my dreams

The True Nature of Love

Scatter to the winds
The last of all your sins
Follow grace unto the place
Where brand new love begins

Give your thanks each day
To gods so far away
Or are they here, so very near?
The players in your play

Coughing up your pride
Casting fear aside
Leaving room for endless bloom
Of the flowers deep inside

They shower you with hope
Tremble as you grope
Blind and wonting, haunted
By so many expectations

Greetings and salutations
We are your grand salvation
Welcome to the truest nature
Of love

The Wizard of Alice

We talk in layman's terms
But we write in the scriptures
Of life and dreams

Any wonder it takes time
To find common ground here

I'm sure we fought
On the same turf
And there are so many
So many others
Have stories

But if you could dance with me
Come sing up the spirit of our past
Together we could shine

The Birthright

Tell me what you see
When you look at me?
The state of my beliefs
Faeries, unicorns and rainbows?

It's true, this is what I need
But not in the way you believe
Not a childish fantasy
A state of play
A fanciful thought
To brighten a rainy day

Look deeper
Feel within
Thundering power
Radiating from realms
Unseen

Magic is a birthright
And I've claimed mine

The New Age

He takes her gently
By the hand
Lifting her eyes
Toward a new age

The golden sun
Life and wonder
Gratitude not so rough
Not so tough

Replaced by insight
A sense of relief
A quick tickle under the ribs
And a strong voice
Telling her
"You know better"

Her heartbeat quickens
Smiles rising up through her

Wracked with humour
She laughs out loud
Awareness
Bursting through the darkness

And the tears that come
Aren't sorrow
But a booming wave of fulfilment
Right here
Right now

This very moment carries her
To heights she's never dreamed
Awash with awe
Baptised with bliss

And the realisation
That nothing that she ever did
Was ever wrong

Every mess was perfect
Every mistake a precept
For a future nepotism
Where thanks and blessings
Are diamonds

"Take heart", he whispers to her
"You're here now"

A New Day Coming

Kept well in the knowledge
That a new day was coming
She kept up the courage
With the strength that she summoned

Destitute and bereft
Taking all that was left
Forced under the covers
Stung by too many lovers

Intrepid feeling
She stepped up
And knowing she was rewarded
She extended her cup
And as it spilled over
She frolicked amidst the clover

The warmth of spring
With songs to sing
And the courage to believe
It may be finally over

Acknowledgements

I need to thank my husband, Aaron, as patient as he is in having his patience tested and taking the reigns for many of the house duties while I have dedicated every waking moment possible to my work. Cheers my love, I appreciate it wholeheartedly. Pretty humble muse that he is.

I also need to thank my beautiful mum, Frances Gillon, who is always there for me to vent to on the phone through all of my ups and downs, and is the most loving, supportive mum I ever could have hoped for.

Thanks to Terry Cooper, for being a truly encouraging force in my life more recently, offering me the invaluable opportunity to be mentored creatively, who has helped me grow artistically, which has paid dividends in all areas of my work.

Also incredible thanks to Jenny, Astrid and Ally at IndieMosh Publishing for their amazing talents and guidance throughout the publishing process, they are a writer's dream come true.

Thank you to all of my friends and family who show me unwavering support on this crazy journey (especially to Alecia Smith who has chipped in with proofreading my work), of course it is all of the love, laughter and epic vibes that you're all sending me that makes this life as amazing as it is. Love and thanks to you all!

About the Author

Catherine Harford is an artist, poet and writer living outside of Sydney, Australia with her husband and her two children. She is the author of the non-fiction work "They Gave Me Truth".

CPSIA information can be obtained
at www.ICGtesting.com
Printed in the USA
BVHW030610161121
621705BV00005BA/285

9 781922 703088